Profiles in American History

The Life and Times of

ABIGAIL ADAMS

Mitchell Lane
PUBLISHERS

P.O. Box 196 · Hockessin, Delaware 19707

Titles in the Series

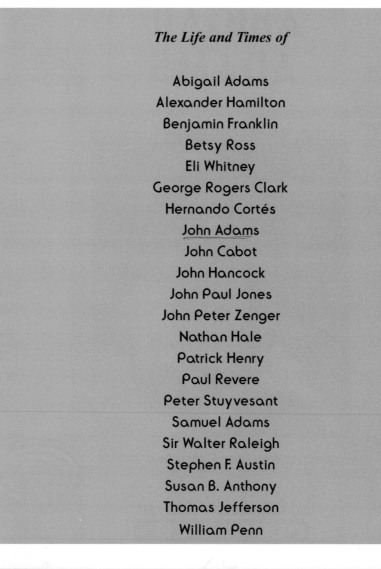

Profiles in American History

The Life and Times of

ABIGAIL ADAMS

Jim Whiting

Copyright © 2008 by Mitchell Lane Publishers, Inc. All rights reserved. No part of this book may be reproduced without written permission from the publisher. Printed and bound in the United States of America.

Printing   1   2   3   4   5   6   7   8   9

Library of Congress Cataloging-in-Publication Data

Whiting, Jim, 1943–
  The life and times of Abigail Adams / by Jim Whiting.
     p. cm.—(Profiles in American history)
  Includes bibliographical references and index.
  Audience: Grades 7–8.
  ISBN 978-1-58415-527-0 (library bound)
 1. Adams, Abigail, 1744–1818—Juvenile literature. 2. Presidents' spouses—United States—Biography—Juvenile literature. 3. United States—History—Revolution, 1775–1783—Juvenile literature. I. Title.
E322.1.A38W48 2008
973.4'4092—dc22

[B]

$20.95

                                                           2007000786

ABOUT THE AUTHOR: Jim Whiting has been a remarkably versatile and accomplished journalist, writer, editor, and photographer for more than 30 years. A voracious reader since early childhood, Mr. Whiting has written and edited more than 250 nonfiction children's books. Representative titles for Mitchell Lane Publishers include *The Life and Times of Franz Liszt, The Life and Times of Julius Caesar, Charles Schulz, Charles Darwin and the Origin of the Species, Juan Ponce de Leon,* and *The Life and Times of John Adams.*
    He lives in Washington State with his wife.

PHOTO CREDITS: Cover, p. 14—Hulton Archive/Getty Images; pp. 1, 3, 6, 17, 20, 24, 33, 34—Library of Congress; p. 19—Jupiter Images; p. 8—National Latino Peace Officer's Association; pp. 9, 32—Corbis; p. 28—Getty Images.

PUBLISHER'S NOTE: This story is based on the author's extensive research, which he believes to be accurate. Documentation of such research is contained on page 46.
    The internet sites referenced herein were active as of the publication date. Due to the fleeting nature of some web sites, we cannot guarantee they will all be active when you are reading this book.

                                                                            PLB

Profiles in American History

Contents

*For Your Information

Abigail Adams was the first woman to be both the wife and the mother of a U.S. president. Her husband, President John Adams, and the country benefited from her intelligence and strength.

CHAPTER 1

A Distinguished First Lady

Abigail Adams scowled as she entered a large and drafty room in the newly built White House. It was cold and damp, and a fire needed to be lit.

She was tired of this house. She was tired of the politics swirling around it. She just wanted to go home to New England.

Abigail made a mental note of the details. She would write about her frustration in a letter home. As the wife of the second president of the United States, she put on a brave face for the American people. Her letters to her family were quite another matter, however.

For many of the First Ladies of the United States—the wives of the presidents—who came after Abigail, the thrill of living in the White House has been great.

Florence Harding was the wife of Warren Harding, who served as president from 1921 to 1923. She said, "I love these beautiful big rooms with their high ceilings, their wide spaces, their polished mahogany furniture, carved deep with memories of Lincoln and the Madisons. . . . I thrill to the thought I am sitting in a chair where they once sat."[1]

In 1963, Jacqueline Kennedy wrote a note to Lady Bird Johnson, the incoming First Lady: "You will be happy here."[2]

Shortly after moving into the White House in 1989, Barbara Bush said, "I thought I'd like being [First Lady], but I never dreamed I would love it."[3]

Laura Bush, who would be First Lady until 2009, has especially enjoyed the holiday season. "Christmas is one of the happiest times here," she said. "Every state is represented with an artist on the tree. And they were very proud to get to see their work on this beautiful White House Christmas tree. . . . The Christmas lights reflect in all the beautiful mirrors that are around here as well as the marble floors, and I think it really is so magnificent."[4]

President George W. Bush and First Lady Laura Bush celebrate Christmas in the White House with Felipe Ortiz (far left) and Roy Garivey of the National Latino Peace Officers Association. Unlike Abigail Adams, Laura Bush has enjoyed living in the White House.

The White House in 1800, soon after President John Adams and First Lady Abigail Adams moved in. The building wasn't complete, and Abigail hated living there.

The first First Lady to occupy the White House had very different feelings. Abigail Adams wrote to her sister Mary, "Mrs. Cotton [Tufts, her aunt] once styled my situation, splendid misery. She was not far from Truth."[5]

Abigail much preferred the comforts of her Massachusetts home. In fact, while her husband, John Adams, was president, she spent more time there than she did with him. In 1798, she was so ill that many people believed she would die. Only an extended period of time at home allowed her to recover.

For nearly a decade, Philadelphia had been the nation's capital. Then the capital moved to Washington, D.C. Construction of the White House wasn't quite complete when the Adamses moved in late in 1800. In many rooms the plaster was still damp.

Abigail hated the new capital. Getting there was bad enough. "[The journey] is very formidable, not only upon accounts of the

[bad] Roads, but the Runs of water which have not any Bridges over them, and must be forded,"[6] she wrote.

Things weren't much better when she arrived. Publicly, no one would have guessed. She was careful to say only good things about her new home. As she told her daughter Nabby, "When asked how I like it, say that I wrote you the situation is beautiful."[7]

Her private letters told an entirely different story.

"Not one room or chamber is finished of the whole," she noted. "It is [only] habitable by fires in every part, thirteen of which we are obliged to keep daily, or sleep in wet and damp places."[8]

As she told her sister, "We have not the least fence, yard, or other conveniences without, and the great unfinished audience room I make a drying-room of, to hang clothes in."[9]

She didn't like the people. The relatively slow-paced way of life in the capital was very different from the bustle and haste to which she was accustomed. It bothered her that few of her new fellow citizens seemed to think being on time for appointments was important.

However, there was a much more unpleasant aspect to Southern life. It was slavery. In 1774, she had written to John, "I wish most sincerely there was not a slave in the province [Massachusetts]. It always seemed a most iniquitous scheme to me—[to] fight ourselves for what we are daily robbing and plundering from those who have as good a right to freedom as we have."[10]

Nearly a quarter century later, moving to Washington gave her firsthand experience of this "iniquitous scheme." She was appalled. She noted that slaves were "half-fed, and destitute of clothing . . . whilst an owner walks about idle. . . . The lower class of whites are a grade below the Negroes in point of intelligence, and ten below them in point of civility."[11]

Getting out of the house for a stroll or to go shopping didn't help her spirits. Today, nearby Georgetown is an upscale neighborhood in Washington. In Abigail's day, it was a different story. "It is the very dirtiest Hole I ever saw,"[12] she wrote.

Their first Christmas in the White House was an extremely sad time for John and Abigail. One of their sons had died just a few weeks earlier.

By that Christmas, the Adamses also knew they would have to move out of the White House soon. In one of the most bitter elections in American history, John had been defeated in his bid for a second term. Abigail believed that Thomas Jefferson, the new president, would usher in a national catastrophe.

Her final letter, written just before departing, said, "My residence in this city has not served to endear the world to me. To private and domestic sorrow is added a prospect of public calamity for our country."[13]

She couldn't wait to get away. She left in early February, 1801, a month ahead of her husband. In all, she occupied the White House for only a short time—less than three months—but she had a tremendous impact on the history of the country.

John Adams did not have an easy job before him when he was elected as the second U.S. president. He followed George Washington, the most respected man in all of American history. Historians believe that Washington almost single-handedly kept the American Revolution alive during its darkest hours. Without him, there would have been no United States of America. The phrase "the father of his country" emerged during his lifetime. The electoral college unanimously elected him as president— something that has never happened again. Washington's vast popularity ensured that he would govern with relatively few problems during his two terms. His equally vast wealth ensured that he could live in a style befitting the nation's highest elected officer.

Adams had none of these advantages. He wasn't a war hero. He wasn't well-off financially. His blunt personal style made him lots of enemies. Even physically, he was at a disadvantage. Washington was a tall, well-built man who towered over nearly everyone else around him. Adams was short, mostly bald, and not nearly as fit.

Far more important, his election marked the beginning of political parties in the United States. Organized opposition often made it hard for him to govern. Thomas Jefferson, his vice president, offered him hardly any support. The presidency

seemed to be a thankless job. He often thought of quitting. It would certainly make his life easier.

Yet Abigail saw beyond his immediate misery and her own. "The President had frequently contemplated resigning," she wrote. "I thought it would be best for him to leave to the people to act for themselves and take no responsibility upon himself."[14]

In other words, resigning would have set a dangerous precedent. It was far better—but also very bitter—to allow the voters to make the decision.

"Of all her works, she admitted, she was most satisfied that she had persuaded John, during his great periods of frustration, to remain in office," notes professor Edith B. Gelles. "In doing so she had served not only John Adams and the nation but history as well."[15]

This admission serves as a summary of her life. In some ways Abigail Adams was very traditional for her era. She believed that a woman's place was in the home. Her main duties were to raise children and support her husband.

In other ways she was definitely not traditional. She had strong opinions on such issues as slavery and women's rights, and she made them known to her husband. Adams regarded her as his intellectual equal. One of her now famous letters urged him to "remember the ladies" as he helped compose the Declaration of Independence.

She also shaped one of her children, John Quincy Adams, into becoming a president. Until the year 2000, when Barbara Bush shared the distinction, she was the only woman who was the wife of one U.S. president and the mother of another.

President Ronald Reagan once said of his wife, Nancy, "In some ways, Nancy and I are like one human being. . . . I'm not sure that a man could be a good president without a wife who is willing to express her opinions with frankness."[16]

John Adams could have said exactly the same thing about Abigail. She established the mold for First Ladies.

Designing and Building Washington, D.C.

When George Washington became the first U.S. president in 1789, the nation's capital was in New York. The Northern states, especially those in New England, wanted it to remain there or to be reestablished in Philadelphia.

The Southern states disagreed. They didn't want the capital so far away. They had an alternative site. Virginia and Maryland would donate some land on the Potomac River. It wasn't far from George Washington's home at Mount Vernon.

The debate raged for several months. It wasn't the only source of disagreement. Each state had incurred considerable debt during the Revolutionary War. Northern states wanted the federal government to pay off those debts. Southern states didn't.

In 1790, the two sides came to an agreement. The capital would be located on the Potomac. While it was being constructed, Philadelphia would serve as the capital. In turn, the federal government would pay all war debts.

The site of the new capital became known as the District of Columbia. It formed a square about ten miles on each side. The capital itself took up only a small part of the site. At first it was named Federal City or Capital City. Soon the name became Washington.

Architect Pierre L'Enfant was hired to design the new capital. He laid out a grid of streets that emphasized two buildings: the Capitol and the President's House. L'Enfant was fired in 1792, before he had finished his plans for the two structures.

Washington and Thomas Jefferson held a competition to design them. The winner of the Capitol competition was Dr. William Thornton. The cornerstone was laid late in 1793. The north wing wasn't completed until 1800, just in time for Congress to meet there. Further construction problems and the burning of Washington, D.C., by the British in 1814 delayed completion of the structure until 1819.

Original Plan for Washington, D.C.

James Hoban designed the President's House. Construction on that was equally slow. Only part of the building was completed by the time the Adams family moved in. It too was burned in 1814. Restoration took three years. During this restoration period it received its distinctive white paint. It became known as the White House.

Abigail Adams as a young woman. Abigail was fortunate to have a father and a grandmother who encouraged her love of learning.

CHAPTER 2

Finding Her Spark

Abigail was born on November 11, 1744. Her hometown of Weymouth was one of the oldest towns in Massachusetts, with a population of about 2,000. Most of the people who lived there could trace their ancestors back several generations. Nearly all of them were small-time farmers and their families.

Abigail's family was different. Her father, William Smith, was one of the town's two ministers. He was also one of the few men in town with a university education. He was well liked and highly respected.

Her mother was Elizabeth Quincy Smith. Quincy was one of the most respected names in Massachusetts. As a minister's wife, Elizabeth had extra obligations beyond taking care of the house and raising the children. She spent a great deal of time visiting sick parishioners.

Abigail had an older sister, Mary, who was born in 1741. After Abigail was born, her parents had two more children: William, born in 1746, and Elizabeth, born in 1750.

Like other girls at that time, Abigail had very little formal education. Her mother taught her the basics of reading and writing. She could also solve simple problems in arithmetic.

Abigail overcame this limitation. Her father had a large library. He encouraged his daughters to browse through it. Abigail was

especially interested in reading her father's books. One reason may have been that her health was not very good. She seemed to be ill more than anyone else in the family, which gave her more time to read.

Abigail had other educational advantages. One was that many intelligent people visited the Smith house. They would discuss issues of the day. The Smith children were encouraged to join in. Several male friends and relatives encouraged her reading habit. They provided her with even more books. She especially enjoyed an English novelist named Samuel Richardson. Richardson's male heroes set a high bar for what Abigail expected from men in her own life. Women were expected to get married and have children. When that happened, women had no legal identity. It was very important to choose a husband wisely.

Some of Richardson's books consisted entirely of letters from different characters to each other. He was reflecting the way that people communicated in that era. Abigail was no exception. From an early age, she wrote many letters to friends and relatives.

Her lack of formal education made her self-conscious about her letter writing. She was afraid that her inability to spell and her difficulties with punctuation might make her appear to be stupid. She needn't have worried.

As historian David McCullough observes, "The strong clarity of her handwriting, the unhesitating flow of her pen across the paper, line after line, seemed at odds with her circumstances. Rarely was a word crossed out or changed. It was as if she knew exactly what was in her heart and how she wished to express it."[1] Historians believe that no other American woman of her era left such an extensive record of the conditions under which she lived.

Late in 1759, Abigail met John Adams for the first time. He was a young lawyer who lived nearby. It was hardly a case of love at first sight.

John, who was nine years older, didn't think that Abigail—or her sisters—were very open or honest. There was probably some truth to this evaluation. As minister's children, Abigail and her siblings had to set an example for other children. They had to

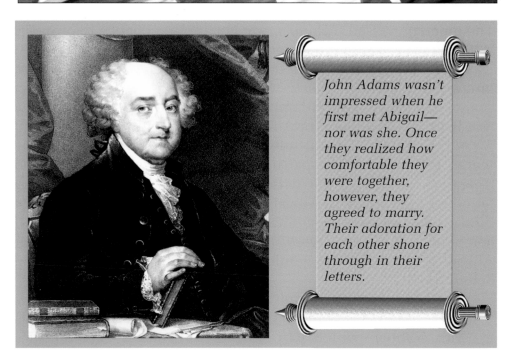

John Adams wasn't impressed when he first met Abigail— nor was she. Once they realized how comfortable they were together, however, they agreed to marry. Their adoration for each other shone through in their letters.

behave properly. They couldn't reveal all their emotions. For Abigail, acting "properly" was especially difficult. Her mother despaired that she was often stubborn and hard to manage. That was one reason Abigail enjoyed spending time with her grandmother Quincy. Her grandmother liked to say, "Wild colts make the best horses."[2] She encouraged Abigail's reading and independent thinking. Abigail could act more freely when she was with her grandmother.

Abigail thought that John talked way too much. She wasn't the only one. He had a tendency to tell everyone his opinions, whether or not they wanted to listen. That wasn't his only flaw. By outward appearances, he wasn't a great catch. He was short, pudgy, and not very good-looking.

The previous year John had begun seeing Hannah Quincy, Abigail's cousin. He knew several other men were also interested in her. He was convinced she liked him the best.

One spring night in 1759, the two of them were alone in a room in her house. He was ready to pop the question. Suddenly the door burst open, and two of their friends came into the room.

The moment passed. Adams never got another chance to propose. Within a year, Hannah married another of her suitors.

By 1761, John's close friend Richard Cranch had become very interested in Abigail's sister Mary. Often John tagged along when Cranch visited the Smith family. It didn't take him long to realize that his first impression of Abigail had been wrong.

Abigail's change in attitude may have taken a little longer. Late that year she wrote a despairing letter to Hannah, who had urged Abigail to come visit her with a "spark," the eighteenth-century term for a boyfriend. Abigail replied that Hannah seemed to think that sparks were "as plenty as herrings."[3] In reality, Abigail complained, "sparks" were very scarce. If Hannah waited for Abigail to find one, she would be very elderly and almost blind before Abigail visited.

Abigail's complaint didn't carry much force. On New Year's Eve, John asked Abigail's sister Mary to deliver a secret message to "Mrs. Nabby," which was Abigail's nickname. That message "ignited the spark."

John no longer felt it necessary to tag along with Cranch to visit the Smith household. He began calling openly on Abigail. One reason for the attraction was obvious. He respected her mind. She respected his. Another was that their personalities were very similar. They both spoke their minds. They felt very comfortable with each other.

When they weren't together, they wrote letters. Some were serious. Others weren't. Once he teased her for sitting with her "Leggs across."[4] Abigail responded that as a gentleman, John shouldn't "concern himself about the Leggs of a lady."[5]

They were married on October 25, 1764. They settled into John's home in Braintree, a few miles from Weymouth. In addition to the house, the property included a farm.

The new couple was joined at a crucial period of United States history. Their marriage endured for more than half a century and weathered some wildly turbulent times.

The Adamses may have hoped for an ordinary life. They were not destined to have one.

Eighteenth-Century Education

Even though Elizabeth Smith had taught her daughter how to read, she thought Abigail spent far too much time with her nose in a book. Abigail wouldn't need all that reading once she was married, she thought.

Elizabeth wasn't alone in regarding too much reading as a waste of time for girls. Education in that era definitely favored boys. Abigail's brother, William, had educational opportunities that she could only dream about.

Many children of both sexes began their schooling in "dame schools." These schools were run by women, often in their own homes. They provided a basic education, primarily teaching youngsters how to read. Most people felt that reading was important. They wanted everyone to read the Bible.

A number of parents preferred to instruct their own children. The quality of this instruction varied widely.

Most towns maintained schools for the children who lived there. Normally boys were the only ones who were allowed to attend. Sometimes girls had the "privilege" of an hour or two of instruction each day. This occurred before or after the much longer periods of lesson time that the boys received.

As a result, biographer Lynne Withey notes, "the vast majority of girls received no formal education past the age of seven or eight; they were doing well if they could read the Bible and write a simple letter."[6]

There was a reason for this apparent indifference. Girls were expected to learn how to take care of a home. Their primary responsibilities in the future would involve cooking, cleaning, taking care of children, and similar tasks. Some well-to-do families hired private tutors for their daughters. These tutors gave lessons in subjects such as music, history, literature, and dancing. Girls with this knowledge would be more interesting wives.

Boys stayed in school longer. Many eventually became apprentices, studying with a master craftsman for a set number of years to learn a useful trade. A very few—especially those who wanted to become lawyers, doctors, and ministers—went on to college. John Adams was one of only twenty-four young men in his graduating class at Harvard College.

Scene in an eighteenth-century school

For Your Information

Riots erupted after the British tried to impose the Stamp Act on the American colonies in 1765. Colonists objected to being taxed without being consulted. Almost exactly a decade later, the dispute would escalate to open war.

CHAPTER 3

In the Shadow of War

France and England had long been rivals in the New World. This rivalry resulted in several indecisive conflicts. In 1754, what became known as the French and Indian War broke out. It was largely fought by British troops, though a number of colonists were also involved.

When it ended in 1763, the French gave up nearly all their territory in the New World. The cost for the British—both human and financial—had been steep. King George III and a majority of the English Parliament decided that the colonies should bear some of the cost. The war had made them more secure. There was only one problem—the king and Parliament came to that decision without really consulting anyone in the colonies.

Parliament passed the Stamp Act in 1765. It was a tax on paper products in the colonies. The colonists were outraged. Many rioted in the streets. They beat up men who tried to sell the stamps.

Adams opposed violence. He wanted to use existing laws to make changes, and he was somewhat successful. The Stamp Act was withdrawn the following year. It was just a temporary respite. The British began levying other taxes. Relations between the colonies and England grew worse. The situation was especially bad in the Boston area. In 1768, British troops occupied the city.

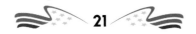

By then the Adams family had begun to grow. Abigail gave birth to a daughter, Abigail Amelia, in 1765. Like her mother, the little girl was nicknamed Nabby. Two years later, John Quincy was born. A second daughter, Susanna, was born in 1768. Sadly, she died shortly after her first birthday. Charles was born in 1770, and in 1772, Thomas rounded out the family.

By the time of Charles's birth, both John and Abigail were deeply committed to the colonists' cause. John's legal practice and his participation in revolutionary politics were increasingly centered in Boston. Several times the family moved back and forth between Braintree and Boston.

The distance was only about ten miles. Abigail wanted to travel much farther. She had been envious when her younger cousin Isaac announced that he was going to England in 1770. Abigail may have been angry with the English government, but she didn't feel the same way about England itself.

John and Abigail Adams lived in Braintree (now called Quincy), Massachusetts, near Boston, where they were close to revolutionary activities. They bought this home, called Peacefield, in Braintree in 1788.

"From my Infancy I have always felt a great inclination to visit the Mother Country, and had nature formed me of the other Sex, I would have been a rover,"[1] she wrote him.

"Roving" was impossible because of her family responsibilities. In addition to taking care of the children, Abigail also had to oversee the farm during John's frequent absences. As the man of the family, John was accustomed to roving. He had to ride the "circuit," taking on legal cases in a number of towns and villages. Sometimes he would be gone for weeks at a time. Abigail understood that these absences were necessary, yet her letters were filled with anguish about how much she missed her "Dearest of Friends and the Tenderest of Husbands."[2] Separation would become one of the dominant themes of the marriage.

A period of even longer separations began in 1774. John became a delegate to the First Continental Congress in Philadelphia. Abigail stayed behind to take care of the farm and the family. John was gone for several months. He and Abigail missed each other a great deal. Their frequent letters helped to ease the pain of being apart.

The following April, the hostility between colonists and the British broke out into open warfare at the Massachusetts towns of Lexington and Concord. John, a member of the Second Continental Congress, quickly left for Philadelphia. The congress had many important decisions to make.

Two months later, Abigail grabbed John Quincy's hand and hurried to the top of nearby Penn Hill. They could see the smoke and hear the thunder of the British bombardment during the Battle of Bunker Hill. It was a firsthand reminder that their lives would never be the same.

Abigail urged her son to remember the date. He did. Nearly seven decades later, he said, "Do you wonder that a boy of seven who witnessed this scene would be a patriot?"[3]

That night, she wrote, "How many have fallen we know not. The constant roar of the cannon is so distressing that we cannot eat, drink, or sleep."[4] The conflict became personal. The fallen included one of their best friends, Dr. Joseph Warren. He was only thirty-four years old.

Engraved by Alexander Hay Ritchie, First Blow for Liberty *depicts the Battle of Lexington on April 19, 1775. The battle was the first conflict of the Revolutionary War, which would last for more than eight years.*

Within a year, the colonists were considering independence. It was a risky venture. England seemed to have all the advantages. John Adams was one of the leading figures in the discussions at the Second Continental Congress. At his suggestion, George Washington was appointed to lead the Continental troops. Adams also became one of the five members of the committee that drew up the formal Declaration of Independence. At that point, Abigail wrote what is perhaps her most famous letter. She fully supported the cause of American independence, and she thought that independence should extend to everyone.

"Remember the Ladies and be more generous to them than your ancestors," she urged. "Do not put such unlimited power

in the hands of the Husbands. Remember that all Men would be tyrants if they could. . . .That your sex is Naturally Tyrannical is a truth so thoroughly established as to admit of no dispute, but such of you as wish to be happy willingly give up the harsh title of Master for the more tender and endearing one of Friend."[5]

She even threatened a revolution of women if her requests weren't honored. It is likely that she wasn't as serious about this part of the letter.

At that time, a husband had a great deal of legal power over his wife. Abigail was pleading for more protection for herself and for other women. Even though it was a private document intended only for her husband, it remains one of the most remarkable pieces of writing by an American woman in her era. Other women may have felt the same way, but it was Abigail Adams who put her feelings on paper, and thereby preserved these feelings for posterity.

"In Practice you know We are the subjects," John replied jokingly. "We have only the Name of Masters, and rather than give up this, which would completely subject us to the Despotism of the Petticoat [being controlled by women], I hope General Washington, and all our brave Heroes would fight."[6]

John was poking fun at her, but Abigail wasn't amused. "I cannot say that I think you are very generous to the Ladies, for while you are proclaiming peace and good will to Men, Emancipating all Nations, you insist on retaining an absolute power over Wives,"[7] she retorted.

She had good reason for insisting on equality. She had done what was considered to be "man's work" while John was gone. She oversaw the operation of the farm, hired and fired men to help out, and even purchased some land. These land purchases had to be carried out in John's name, because women legally couldn't own property. But she did the work.

She also wanted equal educational opportunities for women. She was always self-conscious about her own lack of formal education. She made an important point. In many cases mothers taught their own children. It made sense for mothers to be well educated. That way their children would also be well educated.

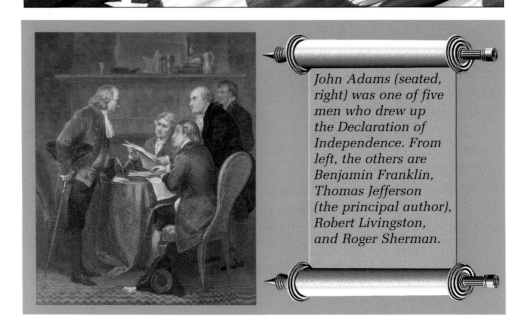

John Adams (seated, right) was one of five men who drew up the Declaration of Independence. From left, the others are Benjamin Franklin, Thomas Jefferson (the principal author), Robert Livingston, and Roger Sherman.

Abigail's thoughts weren't included in the final draft of the Declaration of Independence. It would be decades before women would be recognized as equals. For example, it took nearly 150 years for women to gain the right to vote. Former male slaves were granted the same right 50 years earlier.

Abigail moved on. She had other concerns. A smallpox epidemic was raging through Massachusetts. She had all of her children inoculated. It was a dangerous procedure, but no one in her family fell ill.

Death did strike the family the following year. John was in Philadelphia when Abigail gave birth to a stillborn baby. She named her Elizabeth and buried her. When John returned a few months later, he had good news and bad news. The good news was that he had been selected to go to France to help Benjamin Franklin drum up support for the colonies. The bad news was that the family would be separated. It was too dangerous for Abigail to accompany him, even though she wanted to.

Their previous periods of separation had been painful for them both. This one would be even worse. Except for one brief visit, they would not see each other for more than six years.

The French and Indian War

Britain and France had long been enemies. Several times the wars they fought with each other in Europe carried over into the New World. There was a great deal at stake. Both sides claimed the vast territories that lay between the thirteen American colonies and the Mississippi River.

In 1753, the French began building forts on land that Virginia considered its own. The governor of Virginia ordered an obscure young militia major named George Washington to ask the French to leave. They refused. The following year Washington led an attack on a French scouting party. Historians generally consider that this incident began what became known as the French and Indian War.

Washington's men and their Indian allies won. A wounded French officer was murdered. Washington was falsely accused of the crime.

The French were outraged. Their ire helped to ignite a war in Europe. It began in 1756 and became known as the Seven Years' War. Many European countries were involved on one side or the other.

Back home, Washington became famous. He took over when his British commanding officer and many British troops were killed in an ambush. He led the survivors to safety.

At first the war went badly for the British. The French had more Indian allies than the British did. Slowly the British gained the upper hand. Much of the fighting took place in French-held Canada. The war ended, both in the New World and in Europe, with the signing of the Treaty of Paris early in 1763.

For France, the war was a disaster. The French lost Canada and virtually all of its other possessions in the New World. They retained only two small islands off Newfoundland and two Caribbean islands.

Though the British won, the victory cost them a great deal of money. They had to maintain and supply large bodies of troops both in Europe and in the New World. Paying for the war soon led to conflict with the thirteen American colonies.

A battle in the French and Indian War

A portrait of Abigail's son and future president John Quincy Adams in his late twenties. From a young age, Adams held positions of responsibility. He served as an ambassador, senator, and secretary of state before his election to the presidency in 1824. In later life he was elected to the U.S. House of Representatives, where he was an outspoken opponent of slavery.

CHAPTER
4

Divided by an Ocean

In February 1778, John left for France. He took along John Quincy, "Johnny," who was now ten. John was right about the dangers of the crossing. The ship that carried them across the Atlantic was nearly captured by a British warship. When they arrived, they realized the trip was unnecessary. Overshadowed by Franklin, Adams had almost nothing to do. He felt humiliated.

The situation was just as bad for Abigail. She tried to tell herself that she was making a "patriotic sacrifice" for her country by getting along without her husband. The thought didn't help very much. She rarely heard from John. Letters took months to cross the ocean. If the ship carrying them was captured or sank, they never arrived at all. She had to make many important decisions on her own.

She began a correspondence with a man named James Lovell, who had news about John. Soon Lovell began openly flirting with her. She wrote back that he was being too open and familiar. However, she did not break off the correspondence.

Early in 1779, Lovell sent wonderful news. John was coming home. The situation with Franklin had become intolerable. Abigail was delighted to see him.

Her joy didn't last very long. Shortly after he got home, Congress wanted John to go back to Europe. It seemed that the

war might end soon. John would be an important part of the peace process. He was flattered and quickly accepted.

Abigail knew John would be gone even longer this time. He took both Johnny and Charles with him. The boys didn't really want to go, but their parents agreed that it was important for them to be with their father.

Abigail confessed that she felt almost like a widow. Conditions at home were hard. At one point she didn't hear from John for nearly a year. She began writing to John as "Dear Absent Friend." She also resumed her correspondence with Lovell. The letters never led to anything more serious.

Money was a constant source of worry. She didn't have much income. John frequently sent her gifts from Europe. She had to sell them to make ends meet.

Most of all, she missed his physical presence. At Christmastime in 1780, she wrote, "Separated by a cruel destiny, I feel the pangs of absence sometimes too sensibly for my own repose. . . . I feel myself alone in the wide world, without any one to tenderly care for me, or lend me an assisting hand, through the difficulties that surround me."[1]

Meanwhile, American military forces had suffered a number of losses to the British during the year. The defeat of the Revolutionary cause seemed inevitable.

Almost miraculously, the situation turned around dramatically the following year. Benjamin Franklin's diplomatic efforts bore fruit and the French became much more involved in the American cause. Late that year, Washington and his French allies cornered five thousand British troops under General Charles Cornwallis at Yorktown, Virginia. Cornwallis surrendered. The British government finally decided that the war was not worth the effort. Working out the terms of the formal end of the war took nearly two more years.

The colonies no longer owed their allegiance to the mother country. They became the United States of America.

John remained in Europe. He felt he had other work to do on behalf of his new country. He thought he would become the first U.S. ambassador to Great Britain. It would be a high honor.

Abigail wanted him to come home. At one point, she wrote, "Who shall give me back Time? Who shall compensate to me those years I cannot recall?"[2]

That wasn't the only form of compensation she worried about. John had become involved in Revolutionary politics at the beginning of what would have been his peak earning years. He really put the "servant" in the term "public servant." Servants customarily didn't receive much money from their masters. John was no exception. Yet all around her Abigail saw people making money from the war.

Local busybodies didn't help either. Abigail knew that they were gossiping about her relationship with her husband. "How could a man who really loves his wife stay away so long?" they whispered. "Perhaps he has found someone in France." Abigail knew that he hadn't, but their words still stung her.

Finally John agreed that she would join him. Crossing the ocean was still dangerous, but at least the risk of capture by British warships was over.

She took Nabby. By then, the homesick Charles had returned home. He and Thomas stayed with relatives.

Nearly fifteen years after her letter to her cousin, she finally had the chance for "roving." She had rarely been more than a few miles from home. The voyage was an act of courage. She was traveling without a man—a rarity in that era.

It was a joyous reunion. She also became acquainted with Thomas Jefferson, the U.S. ambassador to France. Both John and Abigail liked him. She even took care of him during an illness.

John received the hoped-for appointment as ambassador to England. The family crossed the English Channel. Five years before, John would have been hanged for such an action. Abigail might have suffered the same fate. Now she could exult. In a letter to Jefferson, she wrote, "An Ambassador from America! Good heavens what a sound. The *Gazette* [a newspaper] surely never announced any thing so extraordinary before, nor once on a day so little expected."[3] In terms of all their separations, something else extraordinary was happening. They would be together for several years.

The Adamses attended many social functions. No detail was too small to escape Abigail's attention in the letters she wrote to her friends at home. At dinner one evening, she noted a woman who "threw herself upon a settee where she showed more than her feet."[4] For the prim and proper New Englander, the sight of a woman's lower leg in public was worth commenting about.

Even more appalling was the woman's lapdog. "When he wet the floor she wiped it up with her chemise. . . . I own I was highly disgusted."[5]

Of course, John had much more pressing work to do. Abigail did, too. Nabby soon fell in love with William Smith, John's personal secretary. They were married in 1786. Abigail had to make all the wedding arrangements. The following year, Nabby provided Abigail and John with their first grandchild, William Smith Jr.

Abigail also had another small child on her hands. Jefferson wanted his eight-year-old daughter Polly to sail to England and stay with the Adams family for a while. The little girl had a difficult ocean crossing. Within a few days, she became close to Abigail. Polly and Abigail would have fond memories of their time together.

Back home, the former colonies were discovering that unity was as difficult to achieve as freedom. The states disagreed about many issues. Adams wasn't there, but he wanted to help. He wrote a book called *Defence of the Constitutions of the Governments of the United States.* Many delegates to the Constitutional Convention in 1787 read the book. After months of debate, they adopted the U.S. Constitution. It contained many of Adams's ideas.

The family followed the book across the Atlantic in 1788. John was having a difficult time as ambassador. Many English people were resentful that the United States had become independent. They took out their resentment on him. John and Abigail also missed their two younger sons. They decided to go home. Finally, John and Abigail thought, they might be able to enjoy a comfortable family life together. They didn't know that once again, politics was about to separate them.

Thomas Jefferson

Thomas Jefferson (left) was born on April 13, 1743, in Albemarle County, Virginia. His father was Peter Jefferson, a planter who owned a great deal of land. His mother was Jane Randolph Jefferson. Her family enjoyed a high social status. Thomas Jefferson took full advantage of the good fortune that his birth had given him.

He attended William and Mary College and then became a lawyer. He entered politics in 1769. He was elected to the Virginia House of Burgesses. The following year he designed his famous home, which eventually became known as Monticello. He built it on land he had inherited from his father. He married Martha Skelton in 1772. They had six children. Only two survived into adulthood. Martha died in 1782.

Most successful politicians are excellent speakers. Jefferson wasn't. He made his reputation because of his writing ability. In 1776, this ability made him the logical choice to write the Declaration of Independence. The document made him famous.

He was elected governor of Virginia in 1779. His most notable act was drafting a law that provided complete religious freedom in Virginia. It ignited a lot of controversy. At that time, no other state or nation allowed this type of liberty.

After the Revolutionary War, he was the U.S. ambassador to France. Later he became George Washington's first secretary of state. In 1796 he ran for president, but lost to John Adams. However, he won enough electoral votes to become vice president. In 1800 he was elected president and won reelection four years later. During his presidency, he oversaw drawn-out negotiations to buy 530 million acres of French territory for just pennies an acre. The deal became known as the Louisiana Purchase, and it was finalized in 1803. It doubled the size of the United States. He organized the Lewis and Clark Expedition to explore the new lands.

After leaving public office, Jefferson retired to Monticello and devoted himself to farming. He also planned the University of Virginia, which opened in 1825. Today the school is regarded as one of the best public universities in the world.

Thomas Jefferson died in the early afternoon of July 4, 1826. It was the fiftieth anniversary of the adoption of the document he was largely responsible for crafting, the Declaration of Independence.

An engraving of Abigail Adams, taken from her official portrait, which was painted while she was First Lady. The artist was Gilbert Stuart, whose image of George Washington appears on the one-dollar bill.

CHAPTER
5

"Her Majesty, the Presidentress"

The Adamses were astonished by their reception when they returned. Many people regarded them as heroes. They bought a new home in Braintree (which was soon renamed Quincy). Called Peacefield, the estate would be their primary residence for the next thirty years.

It wouldn't be their only residence. Under the terms of the new Constitution, a president and vice president would head up the government. Then, as now, presidential elections were decided on the basis of electoral votes. Electoral votes were given out in proportion to the population of each state. Each elector voted for two men. Unlike modern elections, the winner would be president, and the runner-up would be vice president.

To no one's surprise, the popular Washington was the unanimous choice for president. All sixty-nine electors cast one of their votes for him. Adams came in second out of eleven others, with thirty-four votes, to become the nation's first vice president.

At that time, the capital was in New York. The new vice president's wife, the "Second Lady," was happy to move there. Nabby and her husband lived nearby. Abigail's happiness was short-lived. The capital relocated to Philadelphia. She hated living there.

That wasn't the only strain. Family difficulties had become apparent. Nabby's husband, William Smith, turned out to be very irresponsible. He was deeply in debt. John Quincy was still trying to establish himself. Thomas was often ill. Charles had become an alcoholic.

Abigail's husband wasn't very happy either. He had discovered that the vice presidency was an insignificant job. He didn't have very much to do. Washington rarely consulted him.

Abigail disliked Philadelphia so much that she spent most of her time back home. As usual, she and John wrote constantly.

In spite of everything, John ran for president again in 1792. The results were similar to those of the previous election. Washington had one vote from all of the one hundred and thirty-two electors. Adams had seventy-seven, with George Clinton of New York attracting fifty votes. Abigail said she wanted to stay in Quincy. John agreed.

George Washington said he would not seek a third term as president in 1796. That decision heralded the first "real"

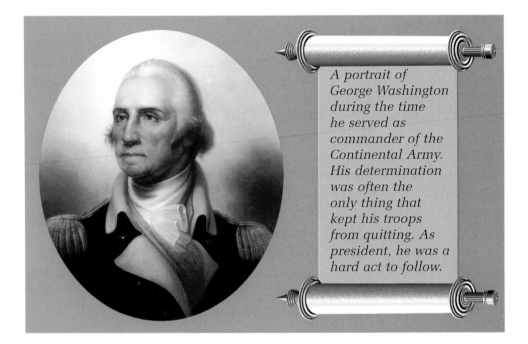

A portrait of George Washington during the time he served as commander of the Continental Army. His determination was often the only thing that kept his troops from quitting. As president, he was a hard act to follow.

presidential election. It also marked the emergence of political parties. As the vice president, Adams was a logical candidate to succeed Washington. He was part of the conservative Federalist Party. But Jefferson also wanted the job. He headed up the more liberal Democratic-Republicans. It was an important election. Some people doubted if the new nation could survive without Washington's personality and influence.

Abigail had mixed feelings. On one hand, she still supported her husband in whatever he wanted to do. On the other, he was in somewhat ill health. She knew that it would be very strenuous for both of them if he won. She was clear about one thing: She still hated Philadelphia. If she became the president's wife, she would spend most of her time in Quincy.

Thirteen candidates received electoral votes. Seventy votes were necessary to win the presidency. Adams had seventy-one. Jefferson had sixty-eight. It had been a bitter conflict. Each side viciously attacked the other. The attacks didn't stop when the votes were counted. The new president found himself under what seemed to be a constant sea of criticism.

Abigail had her own problems to deal with. One was the title by which she would be identified. One man knew of her husband's fondness for the British system of a strong central government. He suggested calling Abigail "Her Majesty." Another wanted her to be known as "The Presidentress." Neither term was flattering. They reflected the anger some people felt about Abigail's influence on her husband. The expression First Lady had not yet been coined.

Tired of the incessant series of attacks, John passed the Alien and Sedition Acts in 1798. It became a crime to criticize the federal government.

Abigail called her husband's critics "traitors to the country."[1] If anything, she supported the two acts even more strongly than did John. She openly rejoiced when two editors who had criticized her husband in their newspapers were sentenced to prison terms. "In any other country they would have been seized long ago,"[2] she commented.

Internal squabbles weren't the only problem facing the country. Foreign affairs were also tricky. The new country soon became caught up in the ongoing dispute between England and France.

Even John's own party turned against him. Federalist Party leader Alexander Hamilton wrote a scathing attack on Adams just before the 1800 election. In spite of all the handicaps, Adams nearly won reelection. He had sixty-five electoral votes. Jefferson and Aaron Burr each had seventy-three. The tie vote went to the House of Representatives. After thirty-six ballots, the House decided in favor of Jefferson.

The election had been even more bitterly contested than the one in 1796. Despite the hostility, there was no violence when Jefferson assumed office. In some ways, the greatest legacy of John Adams's presidency—for which Abigail deserves much of the credit—was the peaceful transfer of power between two political parties that actively hated each other.

Abigail left the White House and went home to Quincy feeling bitter toward the nation and toward Jefferson. Yet being away from the center of power was also a relief. "I have commenced my operations of dairy-woman," she wrote. "Tell Nabby she might see me, at five o'clock in the morning skimming milk!"[3]

There were other compensations. The most important was that finally she and John would no longer be separated. She was surrounded by friends, relatives, and especially her grandchildren. She read a great deal about current affairs. She wrote many letters.

She even had a brief exchange of letters with Jefferson. The two of them had written frequently to each other before their political differences drove them apart. Jefferson's daughter Polly died in 1804. Abigail remembered how close she had felt to Polly seventeen years earlier. Remembering the deaths of her own young daughters, she wrote a letter of sympathy to Jefferson.

To her surprise, Jefferson's response included an explanation of their political differences. He insisted these differences had never had any effect on the respect he had for her or for her husband. "Neither my estimate of your character, nor the esteem

founded in that, have ever been lessened for a single moment," he wrote. "Like differences of opinion existing among our fellow citizens attached them to the one or the other of us, and produced a rivalship in their minds which did not exist in ours."[4]

Abigail felt the wounds were too deep to heal. She mentioned the "former Friendship to which I would gladly return could all causes but mere difference of opinion be removed."[5] She was even more blunt in her final letter. "I will not Sir any further intrude upon your time, but close this correspondence,"[6] she concluded.

Her husband's silence lasted even longer. Early in 1812, at the suggestion of a friend, John Adams finally wrote to Jefferson, who responded soon afterward. The two men became very close, and carried on one of the most famous exchanges of letters in U.S. history.

Abigail had suffered a major blow a few months earlier. Nabby was diagnosed with breast cancer. She underwent a mastectomy. There was no anesthesia to ease the intense pain. Two years later, Nabby died. By then Abigail was becoming accustomed to death. Many of her friends and relatives were gone. Her own health, never robust, continued to suffer.

She tried to stay upbeat. "I always thought a laughing philosophy much wiser than a sniveling one," she wrote to John Quincy. "I am determined to be pleased with the world, and wish well to all its inhabitants."[7]

In mid-October of 1818, she contracted a severe case of typhoid fever. She died a few days afterward. The date was October 28—three days after her fifty-fourth wedding anniversary.

Tributes poured in.

"Though her attainments were great, and she had lived in the highest walks of society and was fitted for the lofty departments in which she acted, her elevation had never filled her soul with pride, or led her for a moment to forget the feelings and the claims of others,"[8] said the Reverend Peter Whitney at her burial service.

The Boston *Columbian Centinel* said, "She was a friend whom it was [Adams's] delight to consult in every perplexity of public

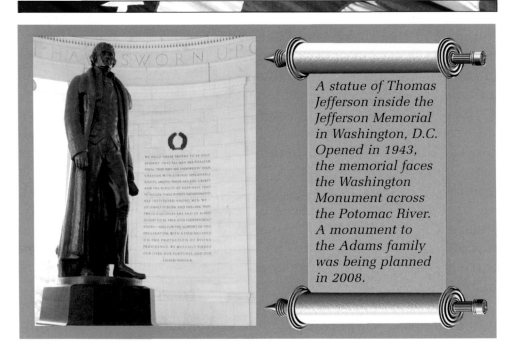

A statue of Thomas Jefferson inside the Jefferson Memorial in Washington, D.C. Opened in 1943, the memorial faces the Washington Monument across the Potomac River. A monument to the Adams family was being planned in 2008.

affairs; and whose counsels never failed to partake of that happy harmony which prevailed in her character."9

Her daughter-in-law Louisa Catherine Adams wrote, "We see her ever as the guiding planet around which all revolved performing their separate duties only by the impulse of her magnetic power."10

John Adams was devastated. Somehow he managed to endure for nearly eight more years. In one of the most fascinating coincidences in American history, both he and Jefferson died within a few hours of each other on July 4, 1826. It was the fiftieth anniversary of the adoption of the Declaration of Independence. They had outlived all but one of the 54 other original signers.

Washington, Jefferson, and Abraham Lincoln all have impressive monuments in Washington, D.C. In 2008, plans were under way for a similar monument to honor Adams. His son President John Quincy Adams was to be included as well.

The monument will also recognize Abigail's achievements. It is a fitting tribute to the woman who was her husband's "Dearest Friend" and primary source of advice.

She is the only First Lady to receive such a high honor.

The Rise of Political Parties

From the very beginning, there was disagreement about the role of the federal government. Some people wanted it to be very strong. Others wanted the states to have more rights. When Washington announced that he would not seek a third term, these disagreements came into the open.

The Federalists wanted a strong federal government, especially in matters involving money. Their strength was in New England. They turned to John Adams. As vice president, he was the logical choice. He won a narrow victory in 1796.

The leader of what became known as the Democratic-Republican Party was Thomas Jefferson. The Democratic-Republicans were centered in the mid-Atlantic and Southern states. They said they were more concerned about "common people" than the Federalists. Jefferson's election in 1800 marked the beginning of a long period of power by the Democratic-Republicans. The Federalists almost vanished. John Quincy Adams even ran as a Democratic-Republican in 1824, but the party soon split apart.

Andrew Jackson took over what became known as the Democratic Party. He said that his primary responsibility was to "the people." He was elected president in 1828 and 1832. Soon afterward, a new party called the Whigs came to prominence. The Whigs opposed Jackson. They thought he had too much power.

The most pressing issue at that time was slavery. The Republican Party emerged in 1854 to oppose it. Abraham Lincoln ran as a Republican in 1860. He took advantage of a split among the Democrats to be elected president. Democrats in the South were bitter about their treatment during and after the Civil War by the Republican Party. For nearly a century they bitterly opposed the Republicans. The region became known as the "Solid South" because it almost always voted Democratic.

The situation changed during the 1960s and early 1970s. Many Southerners didn't approve of the increasingly liberal positions taken by the Democratic Party. Today the South is still "solid." It almost always supports the Republicans.

Abraham Lincoln

Chronology

1744 Abigail Smith is born on November 11 in Weymouth, Massachusetts.

1759 She meets her future husband, John Adams.

1761 Abigail and John begin their courtship.

1764 She marries John Adams on October 25.

1765 The Adamses' first child, Abigail Amelia ("Nabby"), is born.

1767 Their first son, John Quincy ("Johnny"), is born.

1768 The Adamses' second daughter, Susanna, is born.

1770 Susanna dies; their second son, Charles, is born.

1772 Their third son, Thomas, is born.

1776 Abigail sends her "Remember the Ladies" letter to John as delegates to the Second Continental Congress begin drafting the Declaration of Independence.

1777 Abigail gives birth to a stillborn daughter, Elizabeth.

1784 Abigail travels to Paris with Nabby.

1785 She goes to Great Britain with John and Nabby.

1786 Nabby marries William Smith.

1787 Abigail becomes a grandmother when Nabby's son is born.

1788 She returns to Braintree (later renamed Quincy), Massachusetts.

1798 Abigail becomes seriously ill and nearly dies.

1800 She moves to the newly constructed White House in Washington, D.C.; her son Charles dies of alcoholism.

1801 Abigail returns to Quincy after Thomas Jefferson wins the presidential election.

1804 She briefly resumes her correspondence with Jefferson.

1811 Nabby undergoes surgery for breast cancer but dies two years later.

1818 Abigail dies of typhoid fever in Quincy on October 28.

Timeline in History

1706   Benjamin Franklin is born.

1732   George Washington is born.

1735   John Adams is born.

1743   Thomas Jefferson is born.

1754   French and Indian War begins; it ends nine years later with an English victory.

1760   George III becomes King of England; he rules until 1820, the second-longest reign in English history.

1770   Boston Massacre occurs when British troops fire into mob in Boston, killing five colonists.

1775   American Revolution begins with battles of Lexington and Concord.

1776   American colonies formally declare independence from Great Britain.

1783   American Revolution ends with the Treaty of Paris.

1789   U.S. Constitution is formally adopted; John Adams becomes first vice president of the United States; French Revolution begins.

1790   Benjamin Franklin dies.

1797   John Adams succeeds George Washington as U.S. president.

1798   Congress approves Alien and Sedition Acts.

1799   George Washington dies.

1801   Thomas Jefferson becomes the third U.S. president.

1812   The United States and Britian fight the War of 1812.

1825   John Quincy Adams becomes sixth president of the United States.

1826   John Adams and Thomas Jefferson both die on July 4.

1828   Andrew Jackson defeats John Quincy Adams in presidential election.

1848   John Quincy Adams dies.

1920   Women in the United States gain the right to vote with passage of the Nineteenth Amendment to the Constitution.

Chapter Notes

Chapter 1   A Distinguished First Lady

1. Carl Sferrazza Anthony, *American's First Families* (New York: Touchstone, 2000), p. 37.
2. Ibid., p. 361
3. Paul F. Boller, *Presidential Wives: An Anecdotal History* (New York: Oxford University Press, 1998), p. 475.
4. Q&A With First Lady Laura Bush http://www.hgtv.com/hgtv/dc_holidays_occasions/article/0,1793,HGTV_3455_3377314,00.html
5. Phyllis Lee Levin, *Abigail Adams: A Biography* (New York: St. Martin's Press, 1987), p. 310.
6. Edith B. Gelles, *Abigail Adams: A Writing Life* (New York: Routledge, 2002), p. 163.
7. Margaret Truman, *First Ladies* (New York: Random House, 1995), p. 96.
8. Gelles, p. 164.
9. Boller, p. 29.
10. David McCullough, *John Adams* (New York: Simon and Schuster, 2001), p. 104.
11. Ibid., p. 553.
12. Gelles, p. 164.
13. McCullough, p. 559.
14. Gelles, pp. 164–165.
15. Ibid., p. 165.
16. Anthony, p. 77.

Chapter 2   Finding Her Spark

1. David McCullough, *John Adams* (New York: Simon and Schuster, 2001), p. 26.
2. Lynne Withey, *Dearest Friend: A Life of Abigail Adams* (New York: Simon and Schuster, 1981), p. 10.
3. Phyllis Lee Levin, *Abigail Adams: A Biography* (New York: St. Martin's Press, 1987), p. 6.
4. Paul F. Boller, *Presidential Wives: An Anecdotal History* (New York: Oxford University Press, 1998), p. 20.
5. Ibid., p. 21.
6. Withey, p. 8.

Chapter 3   In the Shadow of War

1. Lynne Withey, *Dearest Friend: A Life of Abigail Adams* (New York: Simon and Schuster, 1981), p. 41.
2. Phyllis Lee Levin, *Abigail Adams: A Biography* (New York: St. Martin's Press, 1987), p. 21.
3. Paul F. Boller, *Presidential Wives: An Anecdotal History* (New York: Oxford University Press, 1998), p. 21.
4. David McCullough, *John Adams* (New York: Simon and Schuster, 2001), p. 22.
5. Levin, p. 82.
6. Ibid., p. 83.
7. Ibid., p. 84.

Chapter 4   Divided by an Ocean

1. David McCullough, *John Adams* (New York: Simon and Schuster, 2001), p. 257.
2. Lynne Withey, *Dearest Friend: A Life of Abigail Adams* (New York: Simon and Schuster, 1981), p. 137.
3. Lester Cappon (editor), *The Adams-Jefferson Letters* (Chapel Hill, North Carolina: The University of North Carolina Press, 1987), p. 29.
4. Richard Brookhiser, *America's First Dynasty: The Adamses, 1735–1918* (New York: The Free Press, 2002), p. 42.
5. Ibid.

Chapter 5   "Her Majesty, the Presidentress"

1. Richard Brookhiser, *America's First Dynasty: The Adamses, 1735–1918* (New York: The Free Press, 2002), p. 63.
2. Ibid., p. 50.
3. Paul F. Boller, *Presidential Wives: An Anecdotal History* (New York: Oxford University Press, 1998), p. 19.
4. Lester Cappon (editor), *The Adams-Jefferson Letters* (Chapel Hill, North Carolina: The University of North Carolina Press, 1987), p. 270.
5. Ibid., p. 278.
6. Ibid., p. 282.
7. Phyllis Lee Levin, *Abigail Adams: A Biography* (New York: St. Martin's Press, 1987), p. 480.
8. David McCullough, *John Adams* (New York: Simon and Schuster, 2001), p. 624.
9. Ibid., pp. 624–625.
10. Ibid., p. 625.

Further Reading

For Young Adults

Bober, *Natalie S. Abigail Adams: Witness to a Revolution*. New York: Atheneum Books for Young Readers, 1995.

Ferris, Jeri. *Remember the Ladies: A Story About Abigail Adams*. Minneapolis, Minnesota: Carolrhoda Books, 2000.

McCarthy, Pat. *Abigail Adams: First Lady and Patriot*. Berkeley Heights, New Jersey: Enslow Publishers, 2002.

St. George, Judith. *John and Abigail Adams: An American Love Story*. New York: Holiday House, 2001.

Somervill, Barbara A. *Abigail Adams: Courageous Patriot and First Lady*. Minneapolis, Minnesota: Compass Point Books, 2005.

Works Consulted

Anthony, Carl Sferrazza. *American's First Families*. New York: Touchstone, 2000.

Boller, Paul F. *Presidential Wives: An Anecdotal History*. New York: Oxford University Press, 1998.

Brookhiser, Richard. *America's First Dynasty: The Adamses, 1735–1918*. New York: The Free Press, 2002.

Cappon, Lester (editor). *The Adams-Jefferson Letters*. Chapel Hill, North Carolina: The University of North Carolina Press, 1987.

Gelles, Edith B. *Abigail Adams: A Writing Life*. New York: Routledge, 2002.

Levin, Phyllis Lee. *Abigail Adams: A Biography*. New York: St. Martin's Press, 1987.

McCullough, David. *John Adams*. New York: Simon and Schuster, 2001.

Truman, Margaret. *First Ladies*. New York: Random House, 1995.

Withey, Lynne. *Dearest Friend: A Life of Abigail Adams*. New York: Simon and Schuster, 1981.

On the Internet

Abigail Smith Adams
http://www.whitehouse.gov/history/firstladies/aa2.html

American Experience: John and Abigail Adams
http://www.pbs.org/wgbh/amex/adams/

First Lady Biography: Abigail Adams
http://www.firstladies.org/biographies/firstladies.aspx?biography=2

Get to Know the District of Columbia, Review by Leslie Yezerinac
http://dcpages.com/History/DC_Name_History.shtml

Q&A With First Lady Laura Bush
http://www.hgtv.com/hgtv/dc_holidays_occasions/article/0,1793,HGTV_3455_3377314,00.html

The U.S. Capitol Building
http://www.cr.nps.gov/nr/travel/wash/dc76.htm

The White House
http://www.nps.gov/history/nr/travel/wash/dc31.htm

Glossary

chemise (shuh-MEEZ)
A long, loose dress.

cornerstone (KOR-ner-stohn)
A stone laid at a corner of a building wall, especially during a ceremony; a basic element of something.

electoral college (ee-LEK-tuh-rul KAH-lidg)
A body of electors, especially of the U.S. president and vice president.

ford (FORD)
To cross a body of water by wading.

iniquitous (ih-NIH-kwuh-tus)
Very wicked.

levying (LEH-vee-ing)
Collecting by legal authority.

mastectomy (mas-TEK-tuh-mee)
Surgically removing a breast.

militia (muh-LIH-shuh)
Organized group of armed forces that are called for active duty only in an emergency.

petticoat (PEH-tee-koht)
A skirt worn by women and girls.

posterity (pah-STAYR-ih-tee)
All future generations.

precedent (PREH-suh-dunt)
Something happening for the first time that serves as a way of justifying future behavior.

respite (REH-sput)
Brief rest; temporary relief.

roving (ROH-ving)
Inclined to ramble or travel from place to place.

settee (seh-TEE)
A long couch with a back that is usually wooden.

stillborn (STIL-born)
A child who is dead when he or she is born.

turbulent (TUR-byoo-lent)
Causing unrest, violence, or disturbance.

Index